Bygone South Eastern Steam

Bygone South Eastern Steam

VOLUME ONE

COMPILED FROM THE COLLECTION OF A. R. L. RATCLIFFE

JOHN HALLEWELL PUBLICATIONS LTD
38 HIGH STREET
CHATHAM, KENT

ISBN 0 905540 33 6

BYGONE SERIES (Transport)

South Eastern Steam 2 (*Passenger Rolling Stock*), South Eastern Steam 3 (*Goods Rolling Stock*), South Eastern Steam 4 (*Railway Stations, Events, Linesides*), Bygone Buses (*4 volumes*), Bygone Barges, and Craft of Thames and Medway.
Also available old postcard albums of towns of Kent and Sussex.

Designed and produced by Chambers Green Limited, Tunbridge Wells
Printed in Great Britain by R. J. Acford Limited, Chichester

INTRODUCTION

This is the first volume in our 'Bygone Series' dealing with transport. There is a growing nostalgia for the recent past and to date we have produced seven 'Bygone' postcard albums of towns and villages in Kent and Sussex. Now we add this fine volume on South Eastern steam trains. Mr Ratcliffe has been collecting information on many aspects of Kentish transport and we are pleased that his should be our first transport title. Others we have planned are to cover passenger and goods rolling stock, stations and lineside events, four volumes on South Eastern Buses and Craft of the Thames and Medway.

This is a rapidly expanding series and we welcome suggestions for additions to the range, scope and coverage of the series.

April 1980 *Malcolm John*

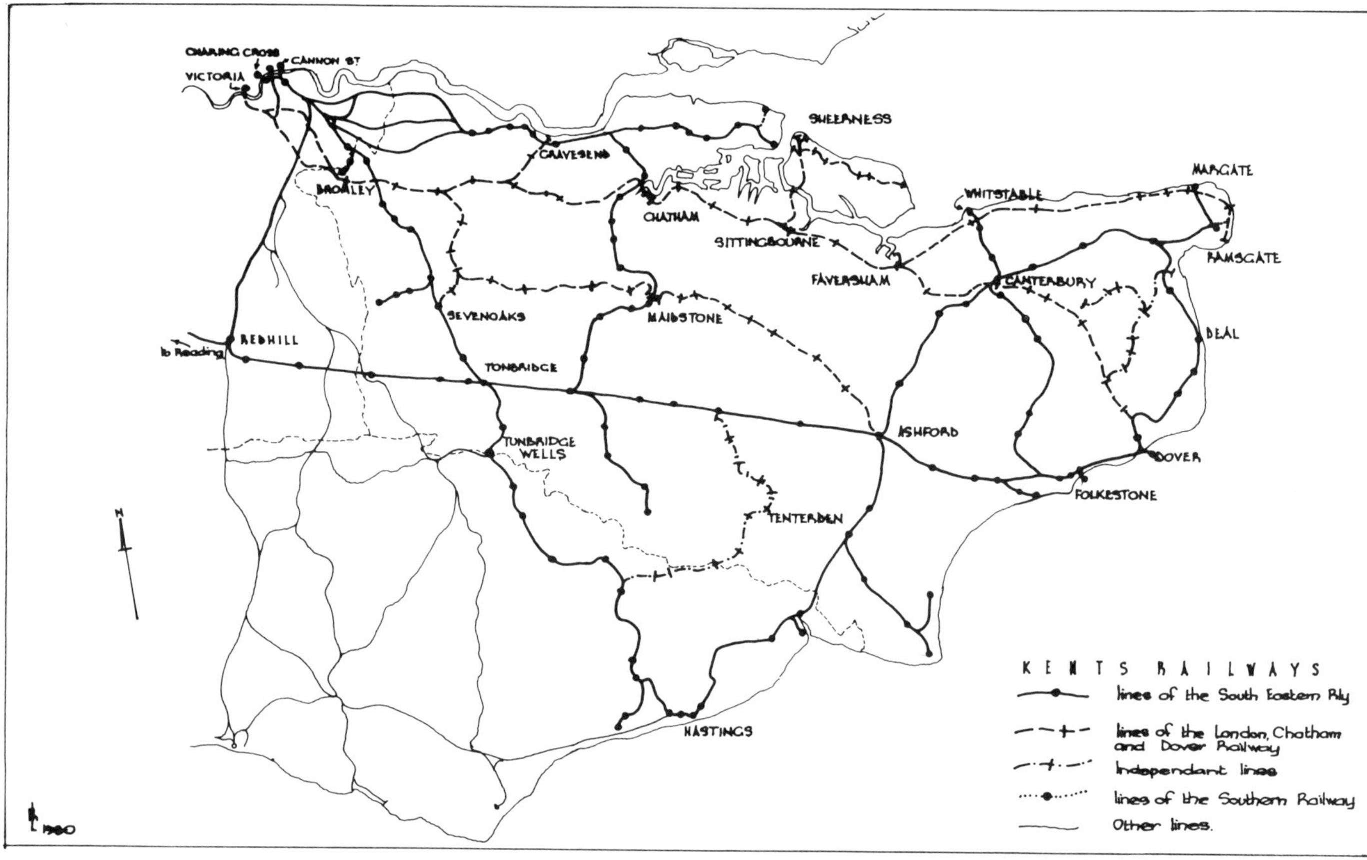
CHARING CROSS
CANNON ST
VICTORIA
SHEERNESS
GRAVESEND
BROMLEY
CHATHAM
SITTINGBOURNE
WHITSTABLE
MARGATE
FAVERSHAM
RAMSGATE
CANTERBURY
SEVENOAKS
MAIDSTONE
DEAL
REDHILL
To Reading
TONBRIDGE
ASHFORD
TUNBRIDGE WELLS
DOVER
FOLKESTONE
TENTERDEN
HASTINGS
N
KENTS RAILWAYS
lines of the South Eastern Rly
lines of the London, Chatham and Dover Railway
Independant lines
lines of the Southern Railway
Other lines.
1980

PREFACE

1980 sees the 150th anniversary of the opening of the first railway in Kent—indeed the first in the world—to carry ordinary passengers regularly in steam hauled trains. The first main line in Kent was opened from London to Dover in 1846 by the South Eastern Railway, and this company and its opponent, the London, Chatham and Dover, had by the end of the 19th century built the majority of the lines we know today. In 1899 they formed a joint operating committee, generally known as the South Eastern and Chatham Railway, and it is the development of motive power from that time until the end of steam in 1961 that is the subject of this booklet. All photographs come from the author's collection, and are credited where the source is known. Especially in this respect thanks are due to the Locomotive Club of Great Britain for their Ken Nunn collection. Where no credit is given, the photographer is unknown, but we do thank these anonymous gentlemen of a bygone age for enabling such a booklet as this to be possible.

A. R. L. Ratcliffe

Edwardian elegance. Wainwright E class 4-4-0 No 157 approaches Chislehurst Junction on the old South Eastern main line. At this point it crossed the LC and D line, and the connecting spurs were one of the first improvements to be instigated by the joint operating committee.

(LCGB Ken Nunn Collection)

Folkestone boat train climbing the 1 in 30 incline from the harbour to the junction station. These trains were exclusively in the hands of Stirling's R—and rebuilt R1—class 0-6-0T until the mid 50s. They worked in pairs at each end of the train, or three in front and one behind.

(LCGB Ken Nunn Collection)

SER 2-4-0 No 221A of Cudworth's 118 class was still used on secondary and branch duties, though the 'A' denotes the duplicate list and imminent withdrawal. She was 36 years old when this photo was taken at Redhill in 1902.

LCDR 2-4-0 No 54 as 513 of the SECR. Designed in 1873 by Martley for the boat train service via Chatham, and one of the 'Europa' class, she survived until 1908.

(LCGB Ken Nunn Collection)

Stirling's O class 0-6-0 were goods engines, but here No 100 works an SER passenger train out of Margate Sands on the now closed line to Ramsgate, where the train would have reversed to continue towards Ashford.

(LCGB Ken Nunn Collection)

Suburban services were usually in the hands of 0-4-4Ts, as here with Q1 class No 354 on a Dartford-bound train near Abbey Wood on 22 June 1919.

(both—LCGB Ken Nunn Collection)

Some of the older engines were rebuilt by Wainwright, including many of Stirling's F class 4-4-0s. Left, an original F, No 91, pulls away from Ramsgate Town with a train composed of typical SE and C 'Birdcage' stock, while above No 110, rebuilt as class F1 heads up the main line past Paddock Wood in 1921 with a train of early army tanks.

730

(both—LCGB Ken Nunn Collection)

SECR expresses. Left, in 1902 brand new Wainwright D class 4-4-0 No 730 accelerates past Rochester with an up express, while above ex LCDR M class 4-4-0 650, built in 1891 to Kirtley's design, stands in the loop at Faversham in the austere grey livery of the post first world war SE & CR.

As a result of the Railways Amalgamation Act 1921, the SE & CR became a part of the Southern Railway from 1st January 1923. Sporting green paint but otherwise unchanged, D class A577 heads for Thanet past Sydenham in South East London in the late 20s.

(LCGB Ken Nunn Collection)

Until electrification in 1939, Maidstone East had a small locomotive shed next to the Brenchley Gardens. Here F1 class A201 receives attention prior to working a train up to Victoria in September 1925.

Wainwright had rebuilt some of Stirling's O class goods engines to class O1, and here 1108 shunts on the quay at Dover in the days just before the outbreak of World War Two.

Wainwright also built 109 of his own design, class C. Intended mainly for goods work, they also were often found on secondary passenger trains, though this picture of 1221 shows it working a heavy freight bound from Tonbridge to Hither Green, London.

(LCGB Ken Nunn Collection)

Wainwright's last design, implemented by his successor Maunsell, was a 4-4-0 classed L. Some were built by the German firm of Borsig, being completed in 1914 just before the outbreak of war, and the class was nicknamed 'Germans'. Here A778 runs through Folkestone Warren with a Dover-bound local.

Various classes of 0-4-4T monopolised the branches, as here at Sharnal Street between Gravesend and Port Victoria, with H class No 1308 on a down train.

SOUTHERN
RIVER ARUN
792

In 1917 the SECR produced prototypes of a 2-6-4T and a 2-6-0 (classed K and N) of very advanced design. More examples of both classes were built after the grouping, though the tank version were all rebuilt in 1927 as tender engines. Left, A792 'River Arun' awaits duty at Brighton, while above N class No 1823 shows the sturdiness of this mixed traffic maid-of-all-work, which could be found all over the system until the early 60s.

The need for more powerful locomotives to cope with the heavier trains of the early twenties resulted in the rebuilding of the D and E classes to D1 and E1, producing a light but most efficient machine. E1 No A165 heads the Dover boat train, composed mainly of Pullman Cars, near Beckenham.

Even with these rebuilds, double heading was often necessary on the boat trains, as shown by this scene at Victoria with D1 No 1727 piloting an F1. On the left a Thanet train waits to leave behind one of Maunsell's U1 three cylinder 2-6-0s.

The next generation of motive power in Kent were the 'Schools', 'King Arthurs' and 'Lord Nelsons' of Maunsell design. The Schools in particular, though only of 4-4-0 arrangement, were most popular with the staff. Here, E901 'Winchester' passes Shorncliffe (now Folkestone West) with an up express.

The 'King Arthurs' were a derivation of a LSWR design, and bore names of knights of the Round Table. 802 'Sir Durnore' brings a Cannon Street to Thanet express through Chislehurst.

Another 'Arthur', No 796 'Sir Dodinas le Savage' runs through Tonbridge with an up express from Folkestone to Charing Cross. These ran non-stop from Folkestone to Waterloo, and were allowed 80 minutes for the journey.

Also at Tonbridge, Stirling B1 class No 1445 shunts a horse box onto a down train. A feature at this time was the locomotive number on the back of the tender.

Electric trains reached Chatham in 1939, but the coastal services remained steam-hauled through to Victoria, as is this up express behind No 763, 'Sir Bors de Ganis'.

No 765, 'Sir Gareth', when new and before fitting of smoke deflectors, pulls out of Dover Marine with a 'Continental Express'.

Another 'up' express from Ramsgate near St Mary Cray with No 765 'Sir Gareth' in charge.

At the same spot, two 4-4-0s are in charge of an 'up' boat train, this one routed via Maidstone East. 1549, as pilot, is a 'D' class on home ground, but the train engine is an immigrant from the 'South Western', a T9 class 4-4-0 No 314.

(LCGB Ken Nunn Collection)

The ultimate power of pre-war days was the 'Lord Nelson' class, which monopolized the boat train workings. The most glamorous of these was the 'Golden Arrow', an all-Pullman train that had been introduced in 1929. Here it passes Bickley Junction behind No 864 'Sir Martin Frobisher'.

In 1946 this train ran again, though by now the 'Nelsons' had gone to the west, and power was provided by one of Bulleid's air-smoothed pacifics of the West Country class, like 21C 125, shown here near Sandling.

Later locomotives of this type were named after personalities and places associated with the Battle of Britain. Here 21C 154 'Lord Beaverbrook' passes Shorncliffe with a continental express bound for Victoria.

(LCGB Ken Nunn Collection)

21C 122 of the earlier West Country class races down Hildenborough bank to Tonbridge with a Charing Cross to Deal express. Sister 21C 123 can still be seen, preserved on the Bluebell Line.

SOUTHERN
1556

Two pictures that show the range of Southern power at the eve of nationalization. Left, Wainwright's P class 0-6-0T No 1556 heads a one-coach train at Tenterden while on loan to the independent Kent and Sussex Railway, and right, new 'West Country' class 21C 127 takes water at Ashford while on a Dover express.

British Railways came into being in 1948, the old Southern Railway becoming the Southern Region. 'Schools' class 'Blundells' sports its new number, 30932, and ownership at Tonbridge, though still painted in malachite green.

The new masters decreed that the 'Schools' were mixed traffic engines, and that they were to be painted black. 30921 'Shrewsbury', so painted and bearing the 'cycling lion' totem, prepares to leave Shorncliffe with an express for London.

(both-LCGB Ken Nunn Collection)

For many years a through train had run between Margate and Birkenhead. In East Kent it ran in two parts from Ashford to Thanet. Left, the part via Canterbury West leaves behind begrimed 30911 'Dover', and above, the part via Dover starts away behind an equally dirty 30916 'Whitgift'.

GOLDEN
ARROW
34083

London's Stewarts Lane depot always produced a clean engine for the 'Arrow' suitably bedecked with flags and a massive 13′6″ long arrow on each side. Left, Battle of Britain class 34083, as yet un-named, rests at Dover Marine shed between trains, and above, sister 34085 sets forth into the evening sun with the 'up' service in Folkestone Warren.

For a while in the early 50s two of the Standard 7MT 'Britannia' class were drafted to Stewarts Lane for this duty. 70014 'Iron Duke' at the same location as the previous photograph brings the Pullmans up from Dover.

Another London-bound continental express in the Warren, this time headed by one of Bulleid's big 'Merchant Navy' class, 35030 'Elder-Dempster Lines'. Five of these Pacifics were allocated to the Eastern Division for the heaviest boat trains at that time.

430
LONDON
NIGHT FERRY
PARIS
21C157

(LCGB Ken Nunn Collection)

Only one passenger service carried through coaches to Europe, this was the 'Night Ferry', which first ran in 1936. In steam days two engines were usually rostered for this, the heaviest of the region's trains. Left, S21C 157 'Biggin Hill' has sole charge of the 'up' train passing Shorncliffe and running via Maidstone East, while above, two 'Battle of Britain' class, 34073 and 34067 pass Faversham on the LC and D route in 1958.

The Age of Steam ended for Kent in 1961, with the implementation of phase 2 of the electrification programme covering the county's routes. Some minor branches were not electrified, and were closed at that time. These included the line to Westerham, where the branch train is seen here with H class 0-4-4T 31553.

The sheds that had housed the iron horses were also closed and demolished. This one was at Gillingham.

Steam can still be found in a few places, thanks to the efforts of railway preservationists. In the south of the county, part of the old Kent and East Sussex railway is now reopened from Tenterden to Wittersham Road. Above, O1 class 31064 leaves Tenterden for Rolvenden before the line's original closure in 1954.

Another early 50s scene on the KESR, this time at Robertsbridge, with 'Terrier' 32678 arriving with a 'mixed' train, conveying passengers (if any) and goods. The bucket always seemed to be a standard fitting on this line.

Until the late 60s, the Bowater Organisation at Sittingbourne operated the largest remaining narrow gauge industrial railway in the country. They even ran passenger trains for the staff, this one awaiting its customers at Ridham behind 0-4-2T Excelsior.

When Bowaters replaced their railway with road vehicles in 1969, they leased part of it to a group of enthusiasts who continue to operate it as the 'Sittingbourne and Kemsley Light Railway' during the summer, as a tourist attraction. Here, 0-6-2T 'Triumph' runs round its train at the Kemsley terminus.

Details of locomotives illustrated in this book

Page	Number (as photographed)	Class	Wheel Arrangement	Built in	Scrapped in	Name	other numbers SR	other numbers BR
6	157	E	4-4-0	12/1907	2/1951		A157/1157	31157
8	221A	118	2-4-0	12/1866	11/1903			
9	513	C	2-4-0	9/1873	6/1908	Asia (till 1892)		
10	100	O	0-6-0	9/1899	8/1926		A100	
11	354	Q1	0-4-4T	4/1891 (cl.Q)	11/1925		A354	
12	91	F	4-4-0	10/1889	12/1925		A91	
13	110	F1	4-4-0	12/1895 (cl.F)	7/1946		A110/1110	
14	730	D	4-4-0	3/1901	3/1951		A730/1730	31730
15	650	M3	4-4-0	9/1891	12/1926		A650	
16	A577	D	4-4-0	9/1906	12/1956		1577	31577
17	A201	F1	4-4-0	11/1885 (cl.F)	11/1933		1201	
18	1108	O1	0-6-0	3/1897 (cl.O)	7/1951			31108
19	1221	C	0-6-0	3/1901	8/1959			31221
20	A778	L	4-4-0	6/1914	8/1959		1778	31778
21	1308	H	0-4-4T	6/1906	12/1962			31308
22	A792	K	2-6-4T	5/1925	7/1928	River Arun		
	(rebuilt as 2-6-0 tender engine of class U, numbered 1792. Scrapped 9/1964 as 31792)							
23	1823	N	2-6-0	5/1923	11/1962			31823
24	A165	E1	4-4-0	1/1908 (cl.E)	5/1959		1165	31165
25	1727	D1	4-4-0	3/1901 (cl.D)	3/1961			31727
26	E901	V	4-4-0	4/1930	12/1962	Winchester	901	30901
27	802	N15	4-6-0	10/1926	6/1961	Sir Durnore		30802
28	796	N15	4-6-0	5/1926	2/1962	Sir Dodinas le Savage		30796
29	1445	B1	4-4-0	7/1898 (cl.B)	2/1948			31445
30	763	N15	4-6-0	5/1925	10/1960	Sir Bors de Ganis		30763
31/32	765	N15	4-6-0	5/1925	9/1962	Sir Gareth		30765

Page	Number (as photo-graphed)	Class	Wheel Arrange-ment	Built in	Scrapped in	Name	other numbers	
							SR	BR
33	1549	D	4-4-0	9/1906	10/1956			31549
	314	T9	4-4-0	5/1901	5/1951			30314
34	864	LN	4-6-0	11/1929	1/1962	Sir Martin Frobisher		30864
35	21C 125	WC	4-6-2	3/1946	7/1967	Whimple		34025
36	21C 154	BB	4-6-2	1/1947	9/1964	Lord Beaverbrook		34054
37	21C 122	WC	4-6-2	1/1946	4/1965	Exmoor		34022
38	1556	P	0-6-0T	6/1910	2/1955			31555
39	21C 127	WC	4-6-2	4/1946	8/1964	Taw Valley		34027
40	30932	V	4-4-0	2/1935	1/1961	Blundells	932	
41	30921	V	4-4-0	10/1933	12/1962	Shrewsbury	921	
42	30911	V	4-4-0	12/1932	12/1962	Dover	911	
43	30916	V	4-4-0	5/1933	12/1962	Whitgift	916	
44	34083	BB	4-6-2	10/1948	6/1964	605 Squadron		
45	34085	BB	4-6-2	11/1948	9/1965	501 Squadron		
46	70014	7MT	4-6-2	5/1951	12/1967	Iron Duke		
47	35030	MN	4-6-2	4/1949	7/1967	Elder-Dempster Lines		
48	S21C 157	BB	4-6-2	3/1947	5/1967	Biggin Hill	21C 157	34057
49	34073	BB	4-6-2	5/1948	6/1964	249 Squadron		
	34067	BB	4-6-2	9/1947	11/1963	Tangmere	21C 167	
50	31553	H	0-4-4T	2/1905	6/1961		A553/1553	
52	31064	O1	0-6-0	11/1896 (cl.O)	5/1958		A64/1064	
53	32678	A1X	0-6-0T	7/1880	10/1963	Knowle (until 1906)	B678/2678	
cover	70004	7MT	4-6-2	3/1951	12/1967	William Shakespeare		
	75	D	4-4-0	3/1903	12/1956		A75/1075	31075

The following industrial locomotives are also shown:

54 Excelsior, built 1905 by Kerr Stuart for Edward Lloyds, Sittingbourne. Now running at Whipsnade Zoo

55 Triumph, built in 1934 by Messrs Bagnalls for the same firm at Sittingbourne, now running on the Sittingbourne and Kemsley Light Railway.

A SOUTH-EASTERN RAILWAY ALBUM

M. John

There have been numerous books on the histories of individual lines or companies operating in the South East area. Now for the first time one book compiles all this information in one volume, giving brief history, development, of each line together with specialist locomotives and many photographs of trains, stations and associated items of interest.

Matching format to *A South-Eastern Bus Album.*
144 pp B/W ills. £4.95

A SAILING BARGE ALBUM

M. John

To match the bus and train albums we are pleased to announce our forthcoming *Sailing Barge Album.* Packed into these 144 pages are hundreds of old photographs and postcard views of these graceful river craft. Gone are the days when they plied our coastline–relive those days with our *Sailing Barge Album.*
(Of associated interest: Sailorman Between the Wars. Life on board these craft between the two world wars.)

144pp B/W ills. £4.95

A SOUTH-EASTERN BUS ALBUM

M. John

This largely pictorial book surveying the history and development of the buses in the South-Eastern traffic area. Brief histories of the Maidstone and District and East Kent, Greenline, Southdown, Kent and Sussex Independents are given as well as 120 pages of glossy photographs. Indexed.

144 pp B/W ills. £4.95

BYGONE BUSES OF KENT AND SUSSEX

(Bygone series)

M. John

Four booklets depicting the fascinating history of the buses in this area: volume I – pre-Second World War; volume 2 – 1945 to 1960; volume 3 – 1960 to present day; volume 4 – various anecdotes, histories and construction details of the buses and garages and accident statistics etc. Each comprising about 50 photographs with accompanying text.
(Produced in co-operation with Maidstone & District and East Kent Motor Services, and M & D and East Kent Bus Club.)

Also see – *South-Eastern Bus Album*

4 Vols. £1.50 each

(front—LCGB Ken Nunn Collection)

Fifty years span these photographs: on the front cover, a down Continental Express passes Grove Park behind D class 4-4-0 No 75 and on the back, the 'Golden Arrow' is in Folkestone Warren in the mid 50s, headed by 70004 'William Shakespeare'.